2 Read With Me!

Forsy
Playt

Written and Illustrated by
Rachel A. DiNunzio

For Emmy, my super friend.

No part of this publication may be reproduced in whole or in part, or stored in a retrieval system, or transmitted in any form by any means, electronic, mechanical, photocopying, recoding, or otherwise, without written permission of the Author. For information regarding permission, write to ContactUs@StudioRADish.com

StudioRADishPress.com

OpenDyslexic by Abelardo Gonzalez is licensed under a Creative Commons Attribution 3.0 Unported License. Based on a work at dyslexicfonts.com.

ISBN: 978-1500599386
Library of Congress Control Number: 2014940639

A Library of Congress Registered Document

Text copyright © 2013 by Rachel A. DiNunzio
Illustrations copyright © 2013 by Rachel A. DiNunzio

All Rights Reserved. Published by Studio RADish Press.

Printed in the USA

Second Edition

2 Read With Me!

Reading Steps®

1 Read To Me! Read aloud to your learner, talk about the story, and make books a fun experience!

2 Read With Me! Work together on sounding out words and connecting the words with illustrations!

3 I'll Read To You! Work together and let your learner take the lead!

4 I'm A Reader! Encourage family reading time! Let your learner read independently while you read too!

For more information about Reading Steps® visit www.StudioRADishPress.com

Imagination Illustration Innovation

Visit StudioRADishPress.com

Every Monday morning, Forsynthia's class worked hard on their weekend journals.

At 10:30, Mrs. Squawk made an exciting announcement!

It is PLAYTIME!

The class was playing a game called, 'city'.
Jackie was dressed up like a chef,
Sue like a doctor,
Mark like a business man,
Paul like a gymnast,
and Frida like a firefighter!

"Sorry Forsynthia, we do not have any costumes for you." Jackie said.

"What do you mean?"
Forsynthia asked.

Well, your ears are
too big for the chef's hat,
your tail will not fit into the suit,

and doctors do not have spots!

The next day, Forsynthia went to school
with her ears taped down,
her tail tucked into her shirt,

and she used her mom's makeup
to cover up her spots!

Forsynthia had it figured out!
She would definitely be able
to play with her friends today!

"CAN I PLAY TODAY!?!"

Today, Jackie had a different excuse.

"Sorry Forsynthia,
but there are no more costumes left
for **you** to dress up in."

At home, Forsynthia sat
at her kitchen table
to do her homework.

Mom noticed
Forsynthia was sad.

"What happened at school today, Forsynthia?" Mom asked.

Forsynthia explained what happened at playtime,

and her Mom listened.

After Forsynthia finished explaining,

Mom said,
"I have an idea!"

Forsynthia and her mom went to the craft store.

They bought fabric, sparkly things, glue, and string.

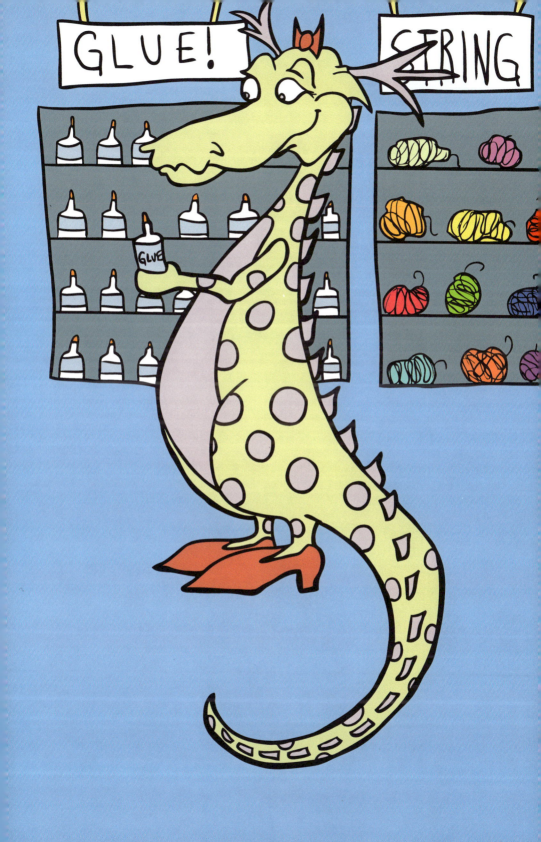

The two worked all night making their top secret project.

They put it in Forsynthia's backpack for school the next day.

The next day at school,
Forsynthia could not
wait for playtime!

Hh Ii Jj Kk Ll Mm

At 10:30, Mrs. Squawk made her announcement.

Forsynthia took out her backpack
and pulled out
her brand new costume.

Forsynthia surprised everyone with her costume; she was a superhero!

Every city needs a Super Forsynthia!

Forsynthia took out her backpack filled with extra pieces of fabric, string, and sparkly things

to help all of her friends
make costumes too!

It turned out to be a SUPER fun day!

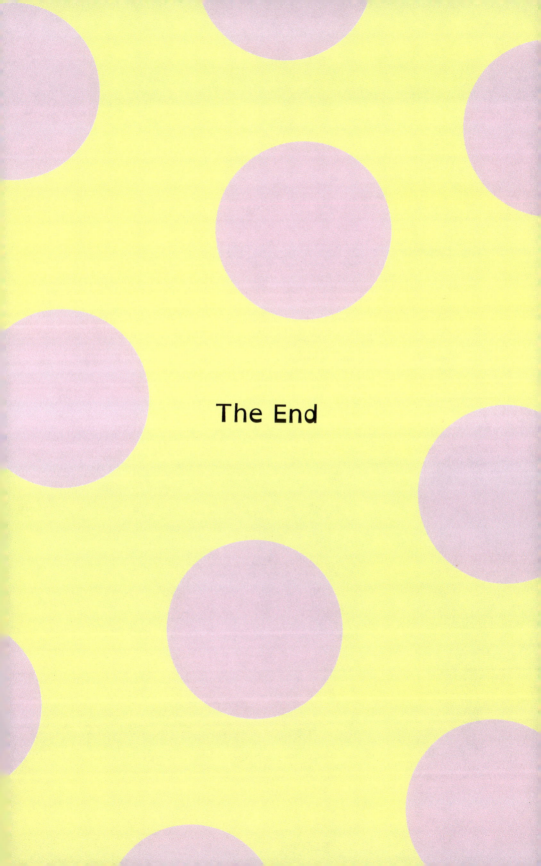
The End

Thank you for reading!

Forsynthia Fits In:

Book #1: Forsynthia's First Day
Book #2: Playtime Troubles

Coming Soon!
Book #3: Girls Can't Play Sports?

For more from the ©Forsynthia Fits In series
visit www.StudioRADishPress.com

CPSIA information can be obtained at www.ICGtesting.com
Printed in the USA
BVIW120217110119
537618BV00011B/60